GIFTED & TALENTED®

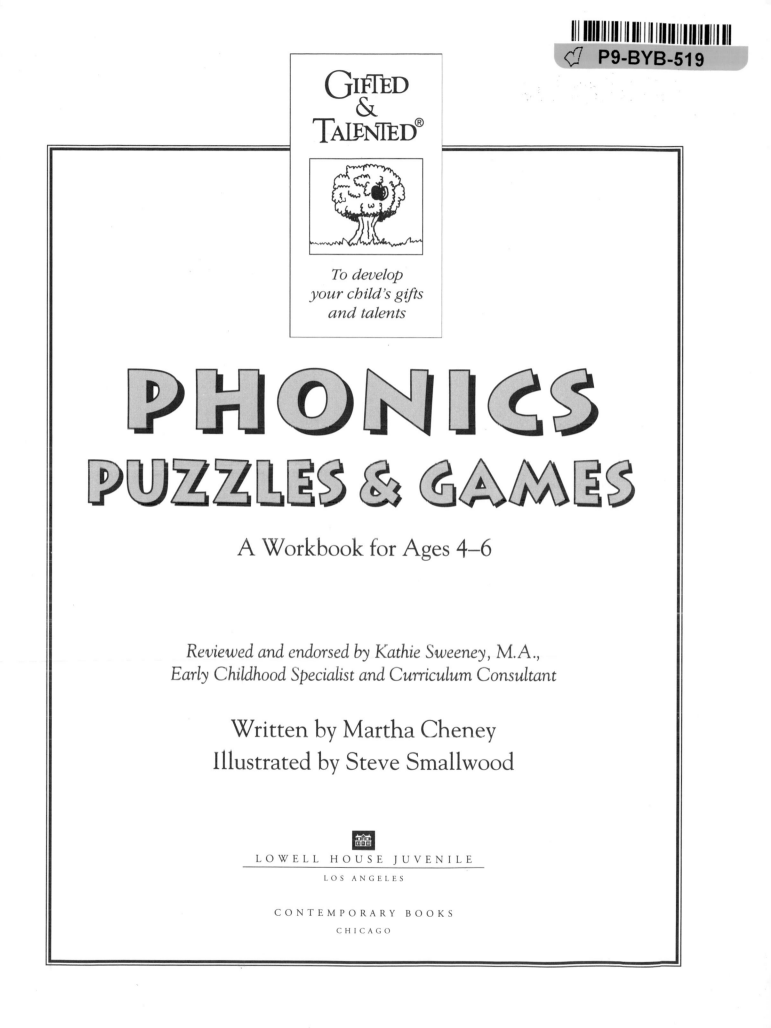

*To develop
your child's gifts
and talents*

PHONICS
PUZZLES & GAMES

A Workbook for Ages 4–6

*Reviewed and endorsed by Kathie Sweeney, M.A.,
Early Childhood Specialist and Curriculum Consultant*

Written by Martha Cheney
Illustrated by Steve Smallwood

LOWELL HOUSE JUVENILE

LOS ANGELES

CONTEMPORARY BOOKS

CHICAGO

Requests for such permissions should be addressed to:
Lowell House Juvenile
2020 Avenue of the Stars, Suite 300
Los Angeles, CA 90067

President and Publisher: Jack Artenstein
Director of Publishing Services: Rena Copperman
Managing Editor: Lindsey Hay
Editor in Chief, Juvenile: Amy Downing
Editor: Jessica Oifer

Lowell House books can be purchased at special discounts when ordered in bulk for
premiums and special sales. Contact Department TC at the above address.

Manufactured in the United States of America

ISBN: 1-56565-568-0

10 9 8 7 6 5 4 3

GIFTED & TALENTED® WORKBOOKS will help develop your child's natural talents and gifts by providing activities to enhance critical and creative thinking skills. These skills of logic and reasoning teach children **how** to think. They are precisely the skills emphasized by teachers of gifted and talented children.

Thinking skills are the skills needed to be able to learn anything at any time. Unlike events, words, and teaching methods, thinking skills never change. If a child has a grasp of how to think, school success and even success in life will become more assured. In addition, the child will become self-confident as he or she approaches new tasks with the ability to think them through and discover solutions.

GIFTED & TALENTED® WORKBOOKS present these skills in a unique way, combining the basic subject areas of reading, language arts, and math with thinking skills. The top of each page is labeled to indicate the specific thinking skill developed. Here are some of the skills you will find:

- Deduction—the ability to reach a logical conclusion by interpreting clues
- Understanding Relationships—the ability to recognize how objects, shapes, and words are similar or dissimilar; to classify or categorize
- Sequencing—the ability to organize events, numbers; to recognize patterns
- Inference—the ability to reach a logical conclusion from given or assumed evidence
- Creative Thinking—the ability to generate unique ideas; to compare and contrast the same elements in different situations; to present imaginative solutions to problems

GIFTED & TALENTED® WORKBOOKS have been written by teachers. Educationally sound and endorsed by leaders in the gifted field, this series will benefit any child who demonstrates curiosity, imagination, a sense of fun and wonder about the world, and a desire to learn. These books will open your child's mind to new experiences and help fulfill his or her true potential.

This book is designed to give children an opportunity to play with and explore the sounds of the letters of the alphabet. This study of the letter sounds is known as **phonics**.

Almost every page asks the child to write or draw in response to the challenge or question presented. This helps to put the task of working with letters in context. The importance of phonics lies in its ability to help us to understand and express language, so in addition to decoding, the child is expected to demonstrate understanding and practice expression. If this proves difficult for your child, don't be afraid to help. Encourage him or her to talk through the responses while thinking them through. If your child has not yet mastered writing, allow him or her to dictate longer answers while you write them. Write slowly, and let your child watch as you form the letters. Together, read back your child's own words.

The activities should be done consecutively, as they become increasingly challenging as the book progresses. Notice that on many pages, there is more than one right answer. Accept your child's response and then challenge him or her to come up with another. Also, where the child is asked to write, remember that the expression of his or her ideas is more important than spelling. At this age, the child should be encouraged to record the letter sounds that he or she hears without fear of mistakes. This process is known as **invented spelling**. If children only write words they know they can spell correctly, they will limit their written expression. Using invented spelling permits your child's spoken vocabulary to be available to him or her for writing.

For example, if your child writes *dnosr* for *dinosaur*, that's okay! Praise your child for the sounds he or she heard. You can encourage the child to listen for the missing vowels as you say the word and write it out so that the child can see the correct form. Just keep the emphasis on his or her success—the letters your child did hear—and not on his or her "error."

Reference charts depicting the sounds of letters appear on the next few pages. Help your child use the charts whenever he or she needs a reminder.

Consonant Chart

b butterfly

h horse

c candle

j juice

d duck

k key

f fox

l leaf

g goat

m moose

n net

v vase

p pumpkin

w window

q quilt

x X ray

r rabbit

y yo-yo

s sandwich

z zoo

t tiger

Vowel Chart

**Short Vowel Sounds
at the Beginning of Words**

**Long Vowel Sounds
at the Beginning of Words**

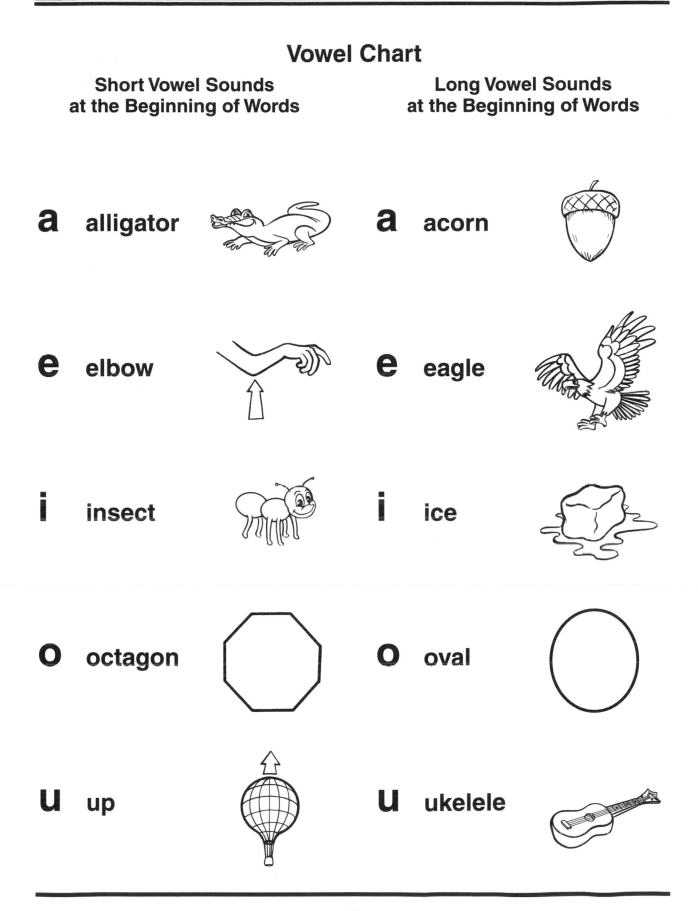

a alligator

a acorn

e elbow

e eagle

i insect

i ice

o octagon

o oval

u up

u ukelele

Short Vowel Sounds
Within Words

Long Vowel Sounds
Within Words

a rat

a rake

e bell

e sheep

i pin

i kite

o box

o coat

u bus

u cube

Use a red crayon to color each square that contains a picture whose name begins with the letter **h**.

For an extra challenge, write the names of the pictures that begin with **h**.

_____   _____

_____   _____

_____   _____

_____   _____

Use a green crayon to color each square that contains a picture whose name begins with the letter **t**.

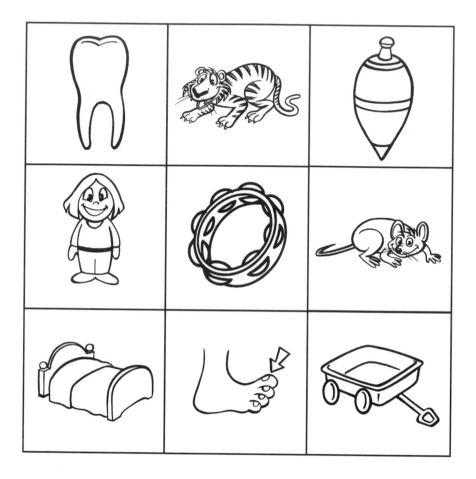

For an extra challenge:

Write the names of the pictures that begin with **t**.

Write the names of the pictures that do not begin with **t**.

Use a purple crayon to color each square that contains a picture whose name begins with the letter **l**.

For an extra challenge:

Write the names of the pictures that begin with **l**.

Write the names of the pictures that do not begin with **l**.

The animals pictured below are missing their tails. Draw a line matching each animal to its tail. Make sure that the letter you see next to the tail is the **last** letter you hear when you say the animal's name.

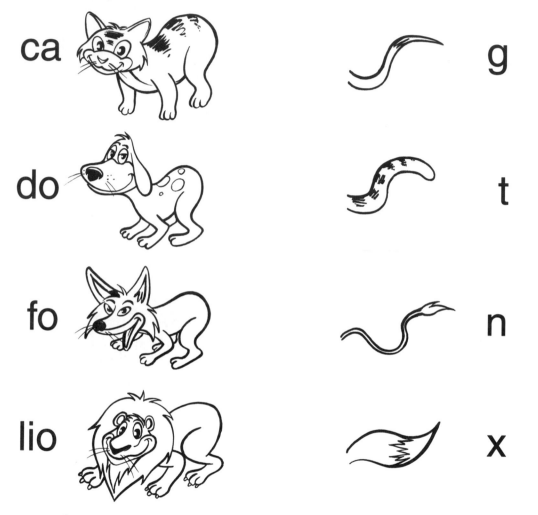

For an extra challenge, think of one or more additional words that end with:

the letter **g** _____

the letter **t** _____

the letter **n** _____

the letter **x** _____

The animals pictured below are missing their tails. Draw a line matching each animal to its tail. Make sure that the letter you see next to the tail is the **last** letter you hear when you say the animal's name.

pi   k

bea   g

shee   r

shar   p

For an extra challenge, think of one or more additional words that end with:

the letter **k** _____

the letter **g** _____

the letter **r** _____

the letter **p** _____

The animals pictured below are missing their tails. Draw a line matching each animal to its tail. Make sure that the letter you see next to the tail is the **last** letter you hear when you say the animal's name.

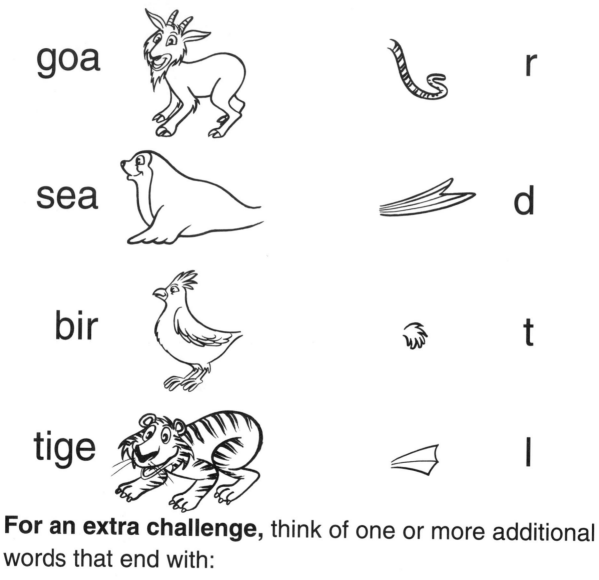

goa

sea

bir

tige

r

d

t

l

For an extra challenge, think of one or more additional words that end with:

the letter **r** _____

the letter **d** _____

the letter **t** _____

the letter **l** _____

Complete the picture to illustrate the sentence in each box.

The man had an apple and a ham sandwich.

Now draw a line under each word in the sentence that contains a short **a** sound.

Jen left the red sled by the tent.

Now draw a line under each word in the sentence that contains a short **e** sound.

Use the letter **i, o,** or **u** to fill in the blank in each word in the boxes below. Use each letter twice. Then draw a picture to illustrate the words you have made.

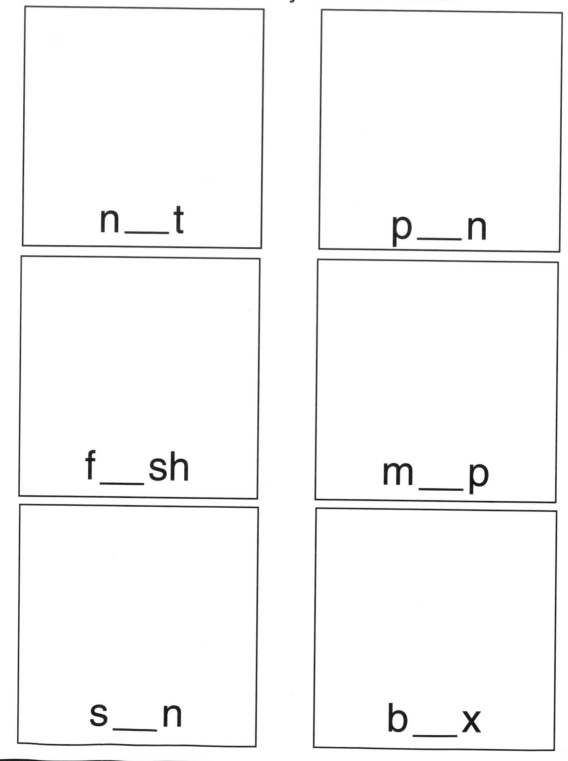

n__t

p__n

f__sh

m__p

s__n

b__x

One letter of each word is missing. Use the picture clues to help you fill in the missing letters.

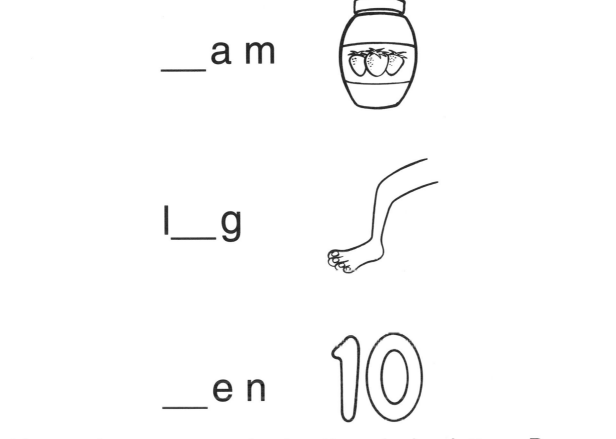

__ a m

I __ g

__ e n

Now make a new word using the missing letters. Draw a picture to illustrate your new word.

___ ___ ___

One letter of each word is missing. Use the picture clues to help you fill in the missing letters.

___ a g

b ___ d

t u ___

Now make a new word using the missing letters. Draw a picture to illustrate your new word.

___ ___ ___

One letter of each word is missing. Use the picture clues to help you fill in the missing letters.

__ i g

b __ g

m u __

Now make a new word using the missing letters. Draw a picture to illustrate your new word.

___ ___ ___

Fill in each blank space with a letter that completes both words in each puzzle.

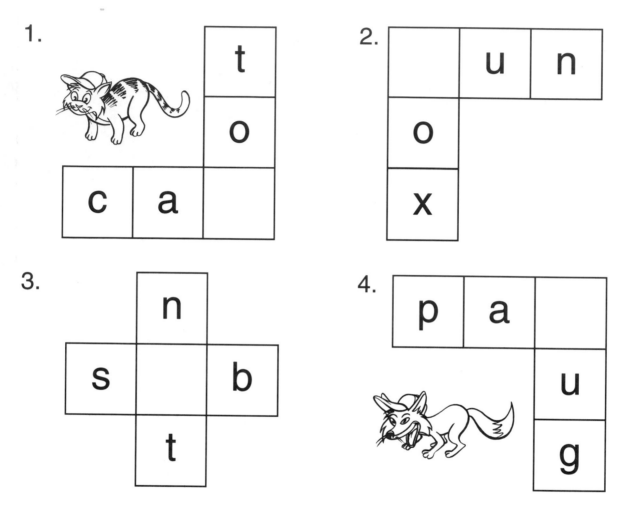

Make a list of all the words that you created.

_____   _____

_____   _____

_____   _____

_____   _____

Now use some of those words to make up a story. Tell your story to a friend or a family member.

Fill in each blank space with a letter that completes both words in each puzzle.

1.
	e	n
o		
p		

2.
	r	
p		n
	p	

3.
h	i	
		i
		x

4.
	m	
r		d
	t	

Make a list of all the words that you created.

_____   _____

_____   _____

_____   _____

_____   _____

Now use some of those words to make up a story. Tell your story to a friend or a family member.

Fill in each blank space with a letter that completes both words in each puzzle.

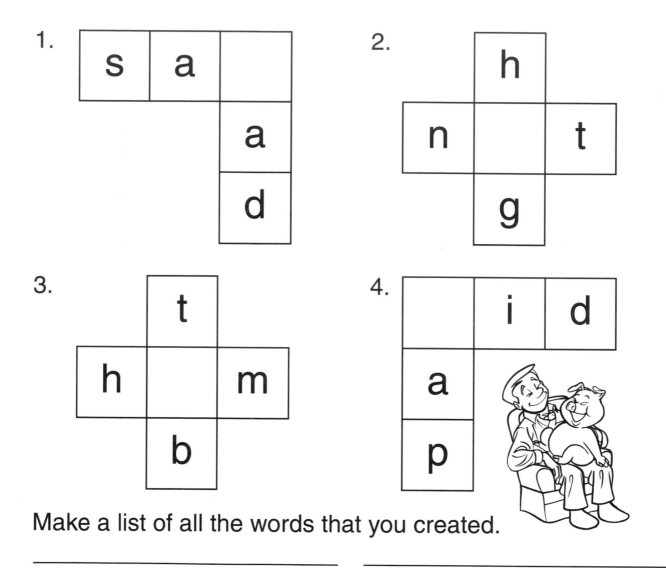

1.

s	a	
		a
		d

2.

	h	
n		t
	g	

3.

	t	
h		m
	b	

4.

	i	d
a		
p		

Make a list of all the words that you created.

_____   _____

_____   _____

_____   _____

Now use some of those words to make up a story. Tell your story to a friend or a family member.

Use the letters on the flowers below to fill in the blank spaces on the butterflies' wings. Use each letter only once. Make sure each word you form makes sense.

For an extra challenge, make up a poem using some of the words on the butterflies' wings.

Look at the letter on the cap that each caterpillar is wearing. What sound does each letter make? Say that sound out loud. Draw one object whose name begins with that sound on each segment of the caterpillar.

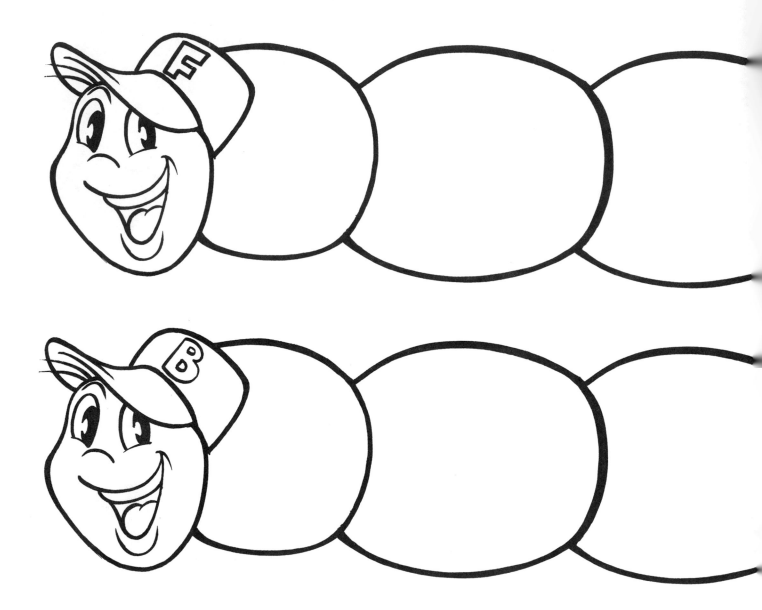

Draw additional segments on a separate piece of paper if you need more space for all your pictures!

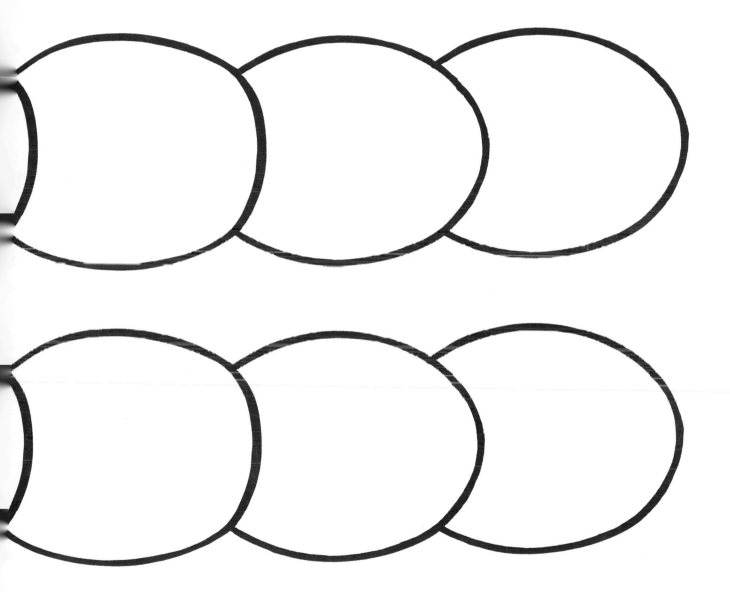

For an extra challenge, create caterpillars using other consonant sounds.

At Farmer Ferguson's Farm, all the animals eat foods that begin with the same sound as their names. Draw a line from each animal to the food it eats.

What other foods could Farmer Ferguson feed his animals?

chicken: _____

cow: _____

horse: _____

pig: _____

Polly is making a patchwork pattern. Use a purple crayon to color each space containing a picture that begins with the same sound as the name **Polly**.
Color all the other spaces yellow.
Now you can see Polly's pattern!

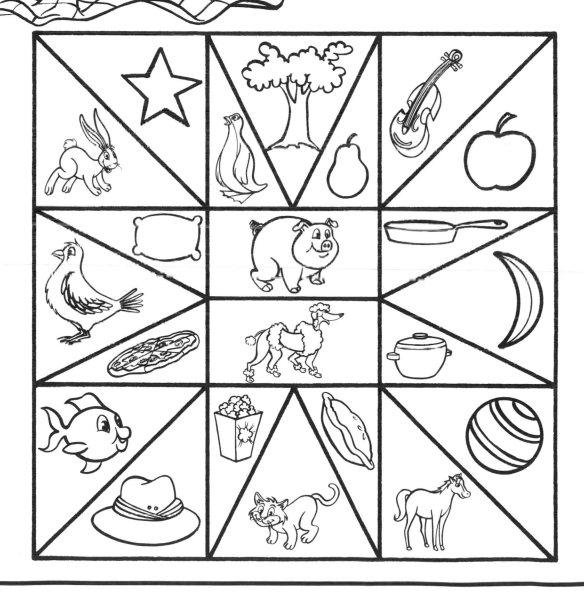

Use number codes to spell telephone words. Look at each three-number code. Then find each number on the telephone below. Use the letters on each number key to spell as many words as you can. Write those words on the lines. **Hint:** The middle letter of your word must be a vowel. The first one is done for you.

8 6 7   _TOP_____

_____

5 3 4 _____

_____

9 2 9 _____

_____

7 4 8 _____

_____

Now write your name.

_____

What numbers on the key pad can
be used to spell your name? _____

Use number codes to spell telephone words. Look at each three-number code. Then find each number on the telephone below. Use the letters on each number key to spell as many words as you can. Write those words on the lines provided. **Hint:** The middle letter of your word must be a vowel.

2 2 3 _____

_____

9 4 4 _____

_____

6 8 8 _____

_____

7 2 3 _____

_____

What is your favorite color?

_____

What numbers on the key pad can be used to spell your favorite color? _____

What letter does the name of this animal **begin** with? ____

Write that letter in the blank space in front of each vowel below.

What letter does the name of this animal **end** with? ____

Write that letter in the blank space after each vowel below.

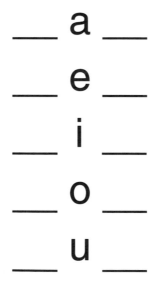

___ a ___

___ e ___

___ i ___

___ o ___

___ u ___

Circle each three-letter combination that spells a **real** word. Then draw a picture on a separate piece of paper to illustrate two of the real words you created.

What letter does the name of this object **begin** with? ____

Write that letter in the blank space in front of each vowel below.

What letter does the name of this animal **end** with? ____

Write that letter in the blank space after each vowel below.

___ a ___

___ e ___

___ i ___

___ o ___

___ u ___

Circle each three-letter combination that spells a **real** word. Then draw a picture on a separate piece of paper to illustrate two of the real words you created.

What letter does the name of this animal **begin** with? ____

Write that letter in the blank space in front of each vowel below.

What letter does the name of this person **end** with? ____

Write that letter in the blank space after each vowel below.

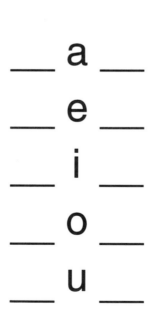

__ a __

__ e __

__ i __

__ o __

__ u __

Circle each three-letter combination that spells a **real** word. Then draw a picture on a separate piece of paper to illustrate two of the real words you created.

Here is a fun consonant chant for you to learn. Notice that all the words in the chant have the same beginning consonant.

Bicky, backy, bumbalina, boopity-bop.

When you have **memorized** the chant, substitute a new beginning consonant for the beginning **b** in each word. When you memorize something, you learn it by heart. Use the consonant chart on pages 5 and 6 if you need help.

____icky, ____acky, ____umbalina, ____oopity-____op.

For an extra challenge, say the chant again and again using each consonant in the alphabet. Try clapping or dancing to the rhythm as you chant.

Draw a line to match each word on the left to the word on the right that has only **one** different letter.

ran	ham
tip	sip
fog	man
Sam	pup
cup	log

Now say each pair of words out loud. What do you notice about each pair? _____

Do these words have short or long vowel sounds? _____

For an extra challenge, make up a poem using some or all of the words.

_____

_____

_____

Draw a line to match each word on the left to the word on the right that has only **one** different letter.

dig   fun

bad   bug

tip   dog

jug   top

fin   bed

Now say each pair of words out loud. What do you notice about each pair? _____

Do these words have short or long vowel sounds? _____

For an extra challenge, make up a poem using some or all of the words.

_____

_____

_____

Use the picture clues below to help you complete the crossword puzzle.

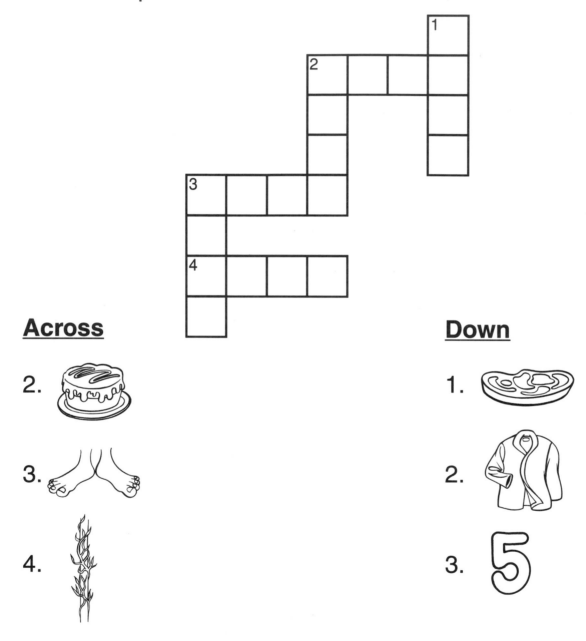

Across

2.

3.

4.

Down

1.

2.

3.

Now say each word in the puzzle out loud.
All the words in the puzzle contain which kind of vowel sound? Circle one: **long short**

Use the picture clues below to help you complete the crossword puzzle.

Across

2.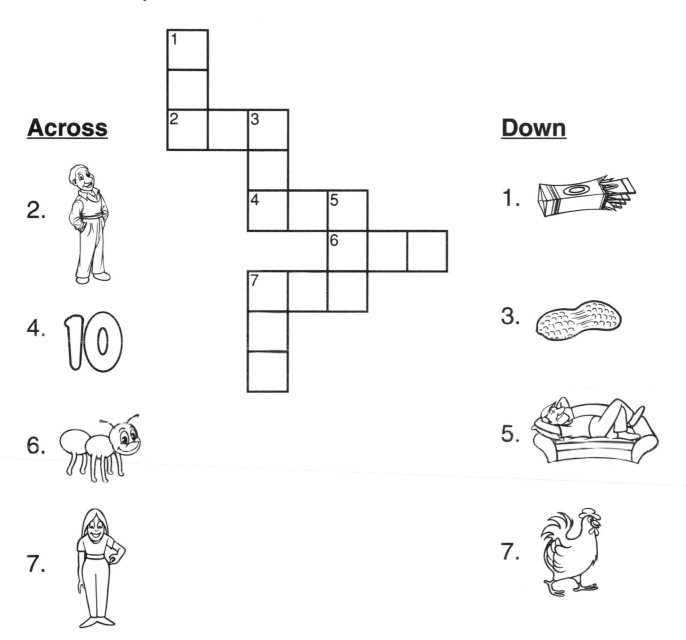

4.

6.

7.

Down

1.

3.

5.

7.

Now say each word in the puzzle out loud.
All the words in the puzzle contain which kind of vowel sound? Circle one: **long   short**

Use the picture clues below to help you complete the crossword puzzle.

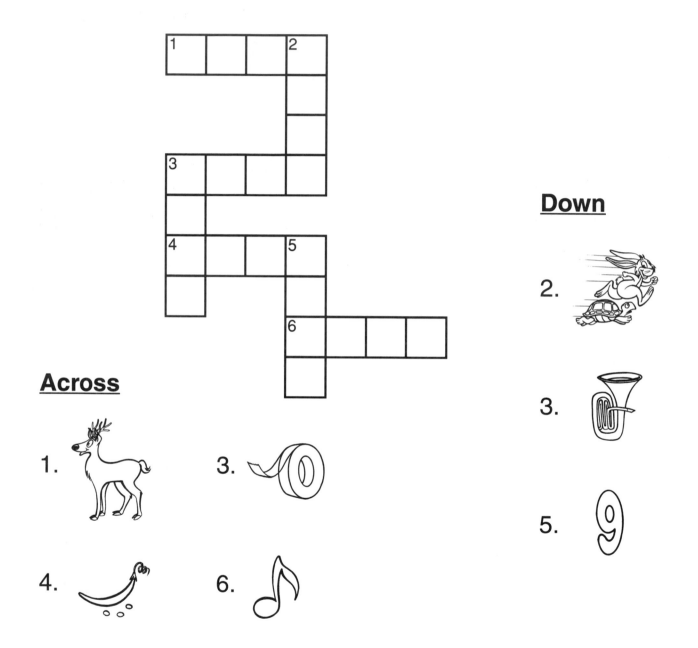

Down

2.

3.

5.

Across

1.

3.

4.

6.

Now say each word in the puzzle out loud.

All the words in the puzzle contain which kind of vowel sound? Circle one: **long short**

All the pictures in this gallery are of objects whose names contain the same long vowel sound. What is it? _____
Add a picture to the gallery. Make sure its name has the same long vowel sound as the other pictures.

Look at all the kids in this park. They are doing lots of fun activities. Draw a circle around each activity whose name has the long **i** sound.

Now tell a story about this park to a friend or a family member. Be sure to include some of the activities whose names have the long **i** sound in your story.

Look at this feast. The name of every food on the table contains the same long vowel sound. What is it? _____ Add a dish to the table. Make sure its name has the same long vowel sound as the other foods on the table.

For an extra challenge, ask a friend or a family member to help you make a list of foods whose names have the short **e** sound. Write the list on a separate piece of paper. Which of these foods is your favorite?

Look at this garden. Draw a circle around all the objects in the garden whose names have the long **o** sound.

Now write a short story about this garden. Be sure to include some of the objects whose names have the long **o** sound in your story.

_____

_____

_____

_____

_____

In a **rebus** sentence, some or all of the words are replaced with pictures. Read the rebus sentence below. What long vowel sound can be heard in each of the words represented by a picture? _____

The _____ wore a _____ and some _____

while she played the _____.

_____

_____

_____

Think of two more words that include that sound. Write them here: _____   _____

For an extra challenge, add another rebus sentence to the story using your new words.

This is a game for two players. Ask a parent or a friend to play with you. To play, you will need one die that you can write on. Ask a parent to write the vowels **a**, **e**, **i**, **o**, and **u** on the die with a permanent marking pen. There should be one vowel on each face of the die. On the one remaining face, draw a star. You will also need two different coins, buttons, or other small objects to use as markers.

1. Both players place a marker on the space marked START.

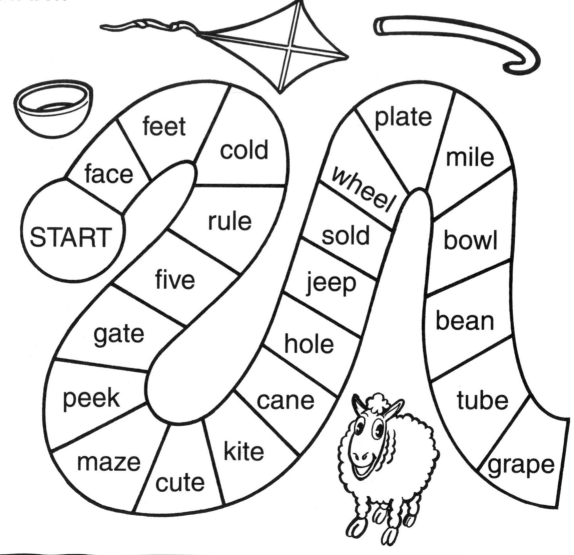

2. Decide who will go first. Let that player roll the die.

3. The player moves his or her marker to the next word on the game board that contains the **long** sound of the vowel shown on the die.

4. Continue playing until one player crosses the finish line.

5. If you roll a star, you lose your turn!

Say each word you land on out loud.

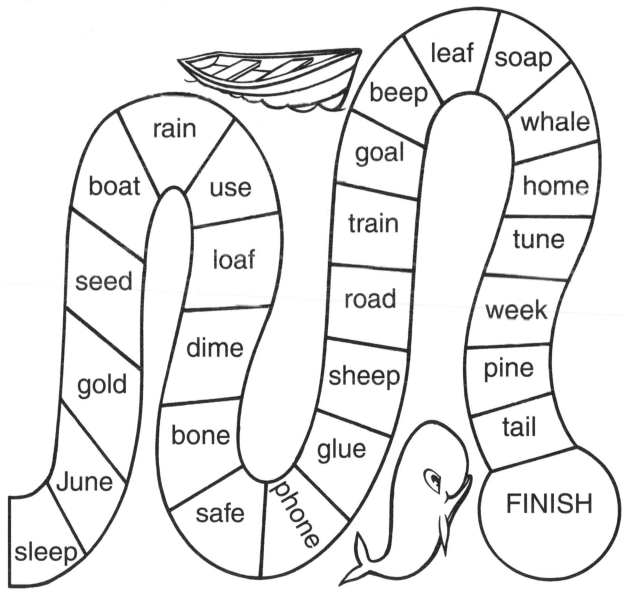

Look carefully at this scene. Circle each object whose name **ends** with the letter **n**.

Make a list of the objects that you found.

_____   _____   _____

_____   _____   _____

_____   _____   _____

_____   _____   _____

For an extra challenge, write a sentence using some of the words from your list._____

_____

Look carefully at this scene. Circle each object whose name **ends** with the letter **g**.

Make a list of the objects that you found.

_____ _____ _____

_____ _____ _____

_____ _____ _____

_____ _____ _____

For an extra challenge, write a sentence using some of the words from your list._____

_____

Find a pair of rhyming words that mean about the same as each phrase below. Then draw a picture in the box to illustrate each rhyme. **Rhyming words** have the same vowel and ending sounds. The first one is done for you.

a large hog

Another word for **large** is ___*big*___.

Another word for **hog** is ___*pig*___.

an angry father

Another word for **angry** is _____.

Another word for **father** is _____.

a very warm pan

A word for **very warm** is _____.

Another word for **pan** is _____.

Find a pair of rhyming words that mean about the same as each phrase below. Then draw a picture in the box to illustrate each rhyme.

a little toy that you can bounce

Another word for **little** is _____.

A word for **a toy that you can bounce** is _____.

a chilly place to swim

Another word for **chilly** is _____.

A word for **a place to swim** is _____.

where a baby bear takes a bath

A word for **baby bear** is _____.

A word for **a place to take a bath** is _____.

Each word below can be changed into a different word by removing just one letter. Read each sentence. Draw an **X** over the letter that must be removed to make the new word. The first one is done for you.

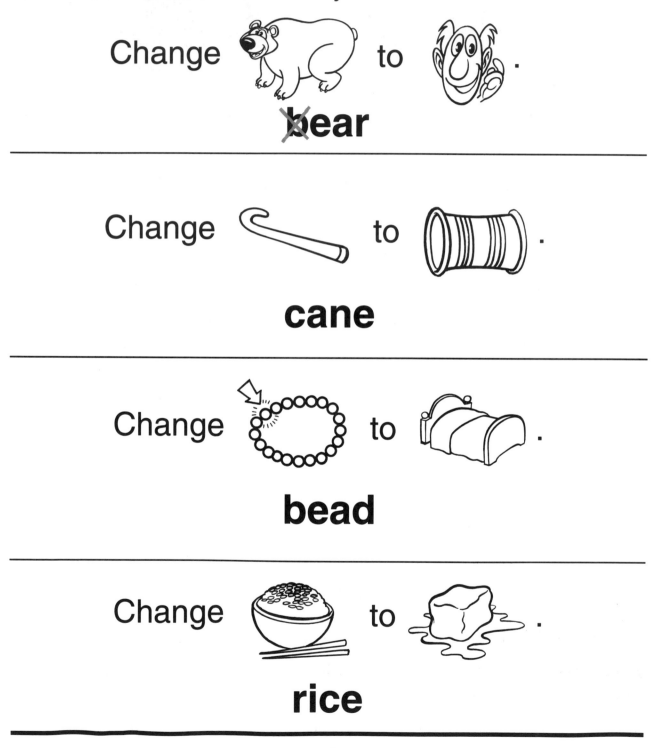

Change to .

X̶ear

Change to .

cane

Change to .

bead

Change to .

rice

Each word below can be changed into a different word by removing just one letter. Read each sentence. Draw an **X** over the letter that must be removed to make the new word.

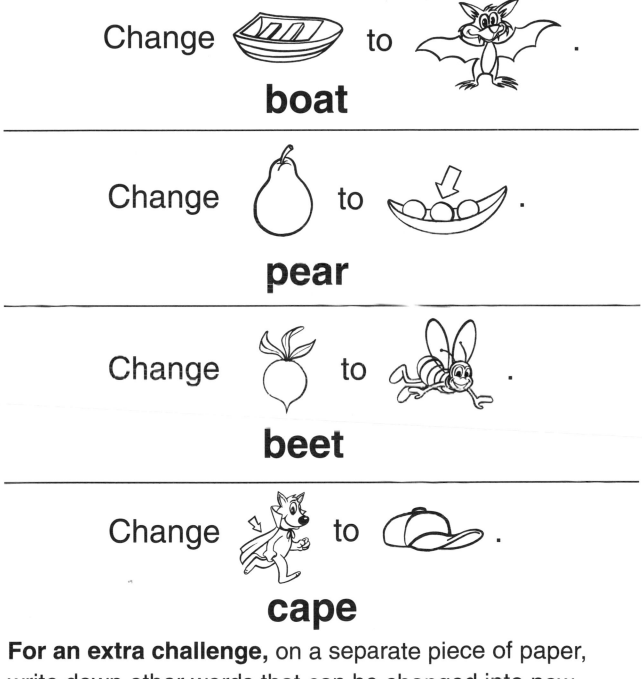

Change to .

boat

Change to .

pear

Change to .

beet

Change to .

cape

For an extra challenge, on a separate piece of paper, write down other words that can be changed into new words by removing one letter.

Look at the pictures on the wheel below. Say the names of the pictures out loud. What letter sound does each of the pictures begin with? Write that letter in the circle at the center of the wheel.

For an extra challenge, make a list of all the words in the wheel on a separate piece of paper. Then add some other words that begin with the same sound.

Look at the pictures on the wheel below. Say the names of the pictures out loud. What letter sound does each of the pictures begin with? Write that letter in the circle at the center of the wheel.

For an extra challenge, make a list of all the words in the wheel on a separate piece of paper. Then add some other words that begin with the same sound.

Draw lines to match each word on the left to the word on the right that has only **one** different letter.

lake   cube

gate   boat

pole   pile

cute   game

beat   cake

Now say each pair of words out loud. Do the words have long or short vowel sounds? Circle one: **long short**

For an extra challenge, make up a poem using as many of the words above as you can. Write your poem on a separate piece of paper.

Draw lines to match each word on the left to the word on the right that has only **one** different letter.

kite	cave
road	bite
beep	blue
glue	beet
cage	read

Now say each pair of words out loud. Do the words have long or short vowel sounds? Circle one: **long   short**

For an extra challenge, make up a poem using as many of the words above as you can. Write your poem on a separate piece of paper.

These five frogs want to cross the lily pond.
Andy can only hop on lily pads that have short **a** words.
Eddie can only hop on lily pads that have short **e** words.
Iggy can only hop on lily pads that have short **i** words.
Ozzie can only hop on lily pads that have short **o** words.
Unky can only hop on lily pads that have short **u** words.
Use a pencil to trace each frog's path across the pond to the other side.

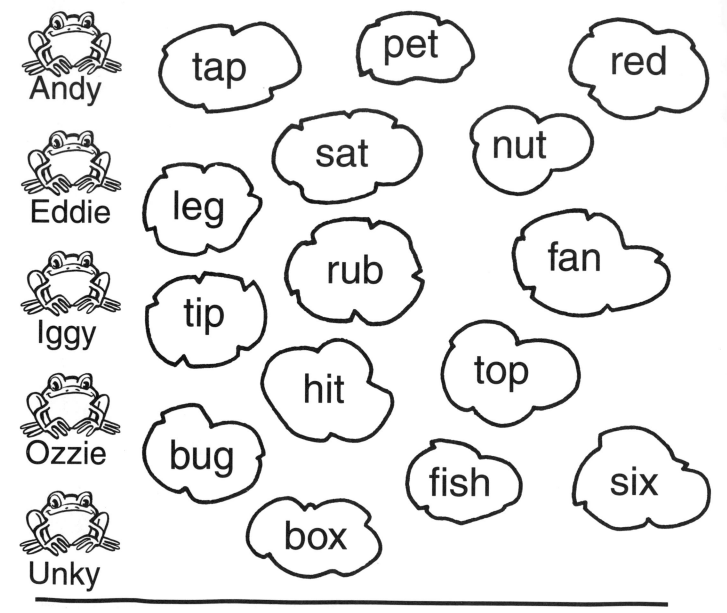

When you are finished, mark each path in a different-colored crayon.

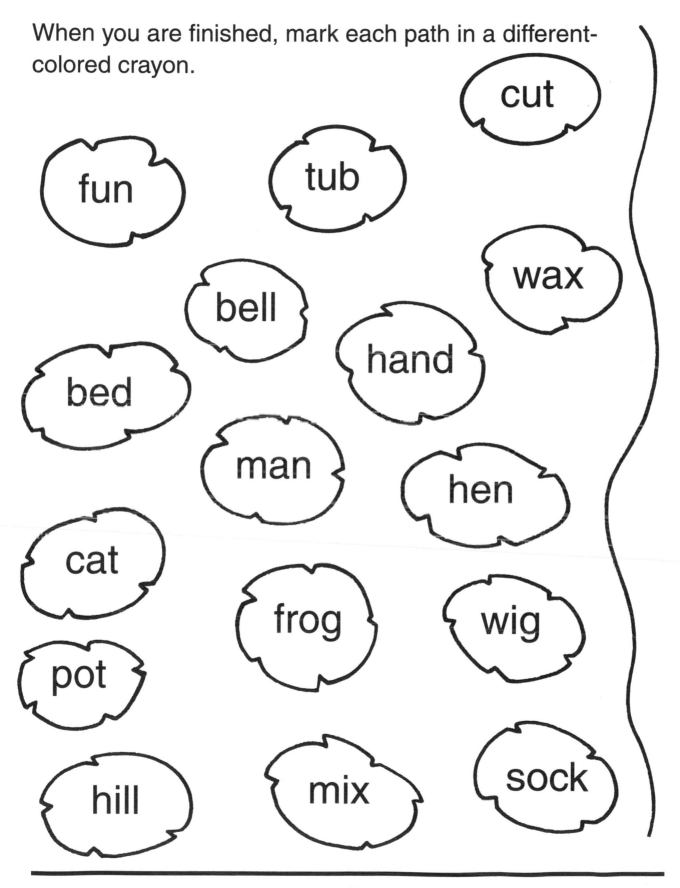

Unscramble the letters on each line to form a word that makes sense.

xim _____

mmo _____

upc _____

igb _____

Write a sentence on the lines below that includes all the unscrambled words.

_____

_____

_____

Now draw a picture to illustrate your sentence.

Unscramble the letters on each line to form a word that makes sense.

upt   _____

gba   _____

ogd   _____

irp   _____

Write a sentence on the lines below that includes all the unscrambled words.

_____

_____

_____

Now draw a picture to illustrate your sentence.

Unscramble the letters on each line to form a word that makes sense.

kibe _____

oagt _____

pjee _____

posa _____

Write a sentence on the lines below that includes all the unscrambled words.

_____

_____

_____

Now draw a picture to illustrate your sentence.

Answers

Page 9

Extra Challenge:

ham	hand
hat	hen
horse	hair
house	

Page 10

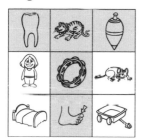

Extra Challenge:

tooth	girl
tiger	mouse
top	bed
tambourine	wagon
toe	

Page 11

Extra Challenge:

leg	duck
lemon	foot
lion	boy
lock	pig
	pumpkin

Page 12

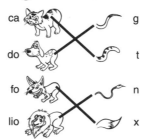

ca — g
do — t
fo — n
lio — x

Extra Challenge:

Possible answers include:
pig, leg, egg, tag, bag
hit, pat, sit, mat, let
man, fan, tan, pen, win
box, ox, wax, mix, six

Page 13

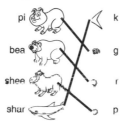

pi — k
bea — g
shee — r
shar — p

Extra Challenge:

Possible answers include:
sink, think, pink, ask, park
hig, rug, bug, hug, rag
car, star, pear, door, her
sip, lip, tip, stop, hop

Page 14

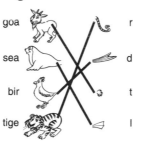

goa — r
sea — d
bir — t
tige — l

Extra Challenge:

Possible answers include:
far, jar, fur, tar, four
hid, lid, sad, bad, red, head
hot, not, dot, goat, night
pail, meal, bell, deal, mail

Page 15

Parent: Child's drawings should include the items in the sentences. The <u>man had an apple and</u> a <u>ham sandwich</u>.
<u>Jen left</u> the <u>red sled</u> by the <u>tent</u>.

Page 16

Most likely answers are: nut, pin, fish, mop, sun, box
Rest of answer will vary.

Page 17

jam, leg, ten
jet
Parent: Picture should reflect child's understanding of word.

Page 18

wag, bed, tub
web
Parent: Picture should reflect child's understanding of word.

Page 19

dig, bag, mud
dad
Parent: Picture should reflect child's understanding of word.

Page 20

Most likely answers are:
1. p and t
2. b and f
3. o and u
4. t and d
List of words might include: top, cap, tot, cat; box, bun, fox, fun; not, sob, sub, nut; pat, tug, pad, dug
Rest of answer will vary.

Page 21

Most likely answers are:
1. p, h, and t
2. i and a
3. m and s
4. e

List of words might include: pen, pop, hen, hop, ten, top; rip, pin, rap, pan; him, mix, his, six; met, red
Rest of answer will vary.

Page 22
Most likely answers are:
1. d and t
2. o and u
3. a and u
4. l and r
List of words might include: sad, dad, sat, tad; hog, not, hug, nut; tab, ham, tub, hum; lid, lap, rid, rap
Rest of answer will vary.

Page 23
Answers will vary but may include: can, keg, sit, rob, mud
Extra Challenge:
Answers will vary.

Pages 24–25
Answers will vary.

Page 26
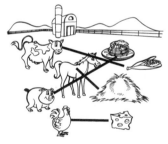

Rest of answer will vary but may include: **chicken:** cherries, chocolate, chili; **cow:** candy, cake, cookie; **horse:** ham, hamburger, honey; **pig:** popcorn, pie, pizza

Page 27

Page 28
534: leg, keg
929: wax, way
748: pit, sit
Rest of answer will vary.

Page 29
223: bad
944: wig
688: nut, out
723: rad, pad, or sad
Rest of answer will vary.

Page 30
h, t
hat, het, hit, hot, hut
Hat, hit, hot, and hut are real words.
Parent: Picture should reflect child's understanding of words.

Page 31
b, g
bag, beg, big, bog, bug
All of the words are real words.
Parent: Picture should reflect child's understanding of words.

Page 32
l, d
lad, led, lid, lod, lud
Lad, led, and lid are real words.
Parent: Picture should reflect child's understanding of words.

Page 33
Parent: Help child substitute consonants correctly, and articulate words clearly. This may take some practice.

Page 34
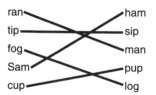

Each pair of words rhymes. The words have short vowel sounds.
Rest of answer will vary.

Page 35

Each pair of words begins and ends with the same letters. The words have short vowel sounds.
Rest of answer will vary.

Page 36

All the words contain long vowel sounds.

Page 37

All the words contain short vowel sounds.

Page 38
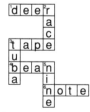

All the words contain long vowel sounds.

Page 39
The vowel sound is long **a**.
Parent: Picture should reflect child's understanding of page.

Page 40

Parent: Answers may vary depending on how child describes what he or she sees in the picture. Guide discussion to include the following: ice skating, riding a bike, sliding down the slide, flying a kite, rock climbing, and horseback riding.

Page 41

The vowel sound is long **e**.
Rest of answer will vary.

Page 42

Parent: Answers may vary depending on how child describes what he or she sees in the picture. Guide discussion to include the following: roses, hose, rope, bone, toad, mole.

Page 43

The vowel sound is long **u**.
Rest of answer will vary.

Pages 44–45

Answers will vary.

Page 46

man, fan, pan, van, hen, pen, ten, pin, sun
Extra Challenge:
Answers will vary.

Page 47

bag, keg, egg, pig, dog, frog, bug, mug, log
Extra Challenge:
Answers will vary.

Page 48

mad dad
hot pot
Parent: Pictures should reflect child's understanding of phrases.

Page 49

small ball
cool pool
cub tub
Parent: Pictures should reflect child's understanding of phrases.

Page 50

can
bead
ice

cane; can
bead; bed
rice; ice

Page 51

boat
pea
bee
cape

boat; bat
pear; pea
beet; bee
cape; cap
Rest of answer will vary.

Page 52

r
Extra Challenge:
run, rug, rat, rain
Rest of answer will vary.

Page 53

s
Extra Challenge:
sun, six, sad, sit
Rest of answer will vary.

Page 54

The words all have long vowel sounds.
Extra Challenge:
Answer will vary.

Page 55

The words all have long vowel sounds.
Extra Challenge:
Answer will vary.

Pages 56–57

Andy's path: tap, sat, fan, cat, man, hand, wax
Eddie's path: leg, pet, red, bed, bell, hen
Iggy's path: tip, hit, fish, six, hill, mix, wig
Ozzie's path: box, top, pot, frog, sock
Unky's path: bug, rub, nut, fun, tub, cut

Page 58

mix, mom, cup, big
Rest of answer will vary.

Page 59

put, bag, dog, rip
Rest of answer will vary.

Page 60

bike, goat, jeep, soap
Rest of answer will vary.

Other

books that will help develop your child's gifts and talents

Workbooks:

- Reading (4–6) $4.95
- Math (4–6) $4.95
- Language Arts (4–6) $4.95
- Puzzles & Games for Reading and Math (4–6) $3.95
- Puzzles & Games for Reading and Math Book Two (4–6) $4.95
- Puzzles & Games for Critical and Creative Thinking (4–6) $4.95
- Reading Book Two (4–6) $4.95
- Math Book Two (4–6) $4.95
- Phonics (4–6) $4.95
- Phonics Puzzles & Games (4–6) $4.95
- Math Puzzles & Games (4–6) $4.95
- Reading Puzzles & Games (4–6) $4.95
- Math (6–8) $3.95
- Language Arts (6–8) $4.95
- Puzzles & Games for Reading and Math (6–8) $3.95
- Puzzles & Games for Critical and Creative Thinking (6–8) $3.95
- Puzzles & Games for Reading and Math, Book Two (6–8) $3.95
- Phonics (6–8) $4.95
- Reading Comprehension (6–8) $4.95

Reference Workbooks:

- Word Book (4–6) $3.95
- Almanac (6–8) $3.95
- Atlas (6–8) $3.95
- Dictionary (6–8) $3.95

Story Starters:

- My First Stories (6–8) $3.95
- Stories About Me (6–8) $3.95
- Stories About Animals (6–8) $4.95

Question & Answer Books:

- The Gifted & Talented® Question & Answer Book for Ages 4–6 $5.95
- The Gifted & Talented® Question & Answer Book for Ages 6–8 $5.95
- Gifted & Talented® More Questions & Answers for Ages 4–6 $5.95
- Gifted & Talented® More Questions & Answers for Ages 6–8 $5.95

Drawing Books:

- Learn to Draw (6 and up) $5.95

Readers:

- Double the Trouble (6–8) $7.95
- Time for Bed (6–8) $7.95

For Parents:

- How to Develop Your Child's Gifts and Talents During the Elementary Years $11.95
- How to Develop Your Child's Gifts and Talents in Math $15.00
- How to Develop Your Child's Gifts and Talents in Reading $15.00
- How to Develop Your Child's Gifts and Talents in Vocabulary $15.00

··

Available where good books are sold! **or** *Send a check or money order, plus shipping charges, to:*

Handy Worksheet

Department TC
Lowell House
2020 Century Park East, Suite 300
Los Angeles, CA 90067
For special or bulk sales, call (800) 552-7551, EXT 30
Note: Minimum order of three titles. **On a separate piece of paper,**
please specify exact titles and ages and include a breakdown of costs, as follows:

··

(# of books) _____	x $3.95	= _____	(Subtotal)	=	_____
(# of books) _____	x $4.95	= _____	*California residents*		
(# of books) _____	x $5.95	= _____	*add 8.25% sales tax*	=	_____
(# of books) _____	x $7.95	= _____	**Shipping charges**		
(# of books) _____	x $11.95	= _____	(# of books) _____ x $1.00/ book	=	_____
(# of books) _____	x $15.00	= _____	**Total cost**	=	_____